# Easy Sheet Music For Oboe With Oboe & Piano Duets Book 1

Michael Shaw

**ISBN: 1517054788**
**ISBN-13: 978-1517054786**

www.mikesmusicroom.co.uk

# Contents

## Introduction

The sheet music in this book has been arranged for Oboe. There are two versions of every piece in this book. The first version is an Oboe only arrangement, the second version is an Oboe and piano accompaniment arrangement. Both versions are for beginners and easy to play. The piano parts in this book can be played on a piano, keyboard or organ.

As well as playing duets with piano in this book you can also play together in a duet or ensemble with other instruments with an easy sheet music book for that instrument. All arrangements are the same and keys are adjusted for B flat, E flat, F and C instruments so everything sounds correct. Piano parts for all instrument books are in the same key.

To get a book for your instrument choose from the *Easy Sheet Music Book 1 with Piano Duets* series. Instruments in this series include, Clarinet, Tenor Saxophone, Alto Saxophone, Trombone, Flute, French Horn and Trumpet.

**Author Page US**
amazon.com/Michael-Shaw/e/B00FNVFJGQ/

**Author Page UK**
amazon.co.uk/Michael-Shaw/e/B00FNVFJGQ/

# Merrily We Roll Along

Oboe

Traditional

# Merrily We Roll Along

Oboe & Piano

Traditional

10
Ob.
Pno.
13
Ob.
Pno.
15
Ob.
Pno.

# Lightly Row

Oboe

Traditional

# Lightly Row

## Oboe & Piano

Traditional

10
Ob.
Pno.
12
Ob.
Pno.
15
Ob.
Pno.

# Lullabye

Oboe

Brahms

# Lullabye

## Oboe & Piano

Brahms

10
Ob.
Pno.
13
Ob.
Pno.
15
Ob.
Pno.

# Barcarolle
## Oboe

Jacques Offenbach

# Barcarolle
## Oboe & Piano

Jacques Offenbach

13
Ob.
Pno.

17
Ob.
Pno.

21
Ob.
Pno.

24
Ob.
Pno.
27
Ob.
Pno.
30
Ob.
Pno.

# Amazing Grace

Oboe

1800 - John Newton

# Amazing Grace

## Oboe & Piano

1800 - John Newton

11
Ob.
Pno.
14
Ob.
Pno.
16
Ob.
Pno.

# The New World Symphony

Largo

Oboe

Antonin Dvorak

# The New World Symphony

Largo

Oboe & Piano

Antonin Dvorak

10
Ob.
Pno.
12
Ob.
Pno.
15
Ob.
Pno.

# Beautiful Dreamer

Oboe

1864 - Stephen Collins Foster

# Beautiful Dreamer

## Oboe & Piano

1864 - Stephen Collins Foster

13
Ob.
Pno.
17
Ob.
Pno.
20
Ob.
Pno.

# Michael Row The Boat Ashore

Oboe

Traditional

# Michael Row The Boat Ashore

Oboe & Piano

Traditional

10
Ob.
Pno.
13
Ob.
Pno.
15
Ob.
Pno.

# When The Saints Go Marching In

Oboe

Traditional

# When The Saints Go Marching In

Oboe & Piano

Traditional

13
Ob.
Pno.
17
Ob.
Pno.
21
Ob.
Pno.

25
Ob.
Pno.
28
Ob.
Pno.
31
Ob.
Pno.

# The Entertainer

Oboe

1902 - Scott Joplin

# The Entertainer
## Oboe & Piano

1902 - Scott Joplin

10
Ob.
Pno.
13
Ob.
Pno.
15
Ob.
Pno.

# About the Author

Mike works as a professional musician and keyboard music teacher. Mike has been teaching piano, electronic keyboard and electric organ for over thirty years and as a keyboard player worked in many night clubs and entertainment venues.

Mike has also branched out in to composing music and has written and recorded many new royalty free tracks which are used worldwide in TV, film and internet media applications. Mike is also proud of the fact that many of his students have gone on to be musicians, composers and teachers in their own right.

You can connect with Mike at:

**Facebook**
facebook.com/keyboardsheetmusic

**Soundcloud**
soundcloud.com/audiomichaeld

**YouTube**
youtube.com/user/pianolessonsguru

I hope this book has helped you with your music, if you have received value from it in any way, then I'd like to ask you for a favour: would you be kind enough to leave a review for this book on Amazon? It'd be greatly appreciated!

Thank You
Michael Shaw

Printed in Great Britain
by Amazon

35458115R00024